SHE CALLS GOD DADDY

Identifying, Improving, and Overcoming Deficiencies Through Scriptures

SHE CALLS GOD DADDY WORKBOOK

DR. ARIE LOUISE FORSHE, PH.D., MSW

WESTBOW
PRESS®
A DIVISION OF THOMAS NELSON
& ZONDERVAN

WestBow Press books may be ordered through booksellers or by contacting:

WestBow Press
A Division of Thomas Nelson & Zondervan
1663 Liberty Drive
Bloomington, IN 47403
www.westbowpress.com
1 (866) 928-1240

ISBN: 978-1-5127-3286-3 (sc)

Library of Congress Control Number: 2016903185

Print information available on the last page.

WestBow Press rev. date: 07/22/2016

CONTENTS

Dedication vii

Forward xi

Chapter 1 I Didn't Know That God Wanted To Be My Daddy? 1

Chapter 2 My Daddy Is Awesome...5

Chapter 3 My Daddy Let Me Know Why I Am Suffering 9

Chapter 4 My Self-esteem Comes from My Daddy. 23

Chapter 5 DidYou know That My Daddy Told Me That I'm Unique?...........29

Chapter 6 I Inherited Some of My Daddy's Power 37

Chapter 7 Who Is My Role Model? My Daddy...............................41

Chapter 8   Did You Know That My Daddy Said Affirmations Are
            Spiritual Food For the Soul? 45

Chapter 9 Did You Read Some of My Daddy's Life Lessons from the
            Biblical Time that My Daddy Left Behind?........................51

Chapter 10 My Dad Wants You to Enjoy the Fruits of the Spirit....................55

Chapter 11 I have Some of My Daddy's Glory 61

Chapter 12 Leadership...71

Chapter 13 What happened?...79

Chapter 14 A Life Without the Balance 87

Chapter 15 Letters 93

DEDICATION

This book is dedicated to the highest God, My Daddy.

This book is also available in Spanish.

G
O
D
is
MY Daddy

Pastor, Dr. Louise Forshe Ph.d, MSW

FORWARD

This book is designed to help pastors, counselors, social workers, and as I think of ordinary people. It will help you with building your self-esteem through God's principles and values. The workbook can also be used to help you with your spiritual growth. Anyone can use this workbook that wants to improve their weakness.

This book is for daughters and fathers who are deceased. The book is also for girls who feel they did not get the unconditional love of their father. It is a book that can also be use for women with broken spirit. The book will heal your emotions and lift your spirit, and self-esteem.

This book is built on Biblical Principles and their values.

CHAPTER ONE

I Didn't Know That God Wanted To Be My Daddy?

January 3, 2015

G

O

D

I AM HAPPY.
THANK YOU DADDY
FOR
LOVING ME AND GUIDING ME.
Thanks - ABBA - Father
Mark 14:36
Romans 8:15
Galatians 4: 6

CHAPTER TWO

My Daddy Is Awesome

I have called God daddy for six days. God has shown me great affection as my Daddy since 20th of January. I had a big meeting with my daddy. I went to bed thinking I feel special because God is my daddy.

Dr. Arie Louise Forshe, Ph.D., MSW

Thank You Daddy for

YOUR PATIENCE   YOUR GRACE

YOUR KINDNESS   YOUR MERCY

YOUR UNDERSTANDING

YOUR CORRECTION

YOUR DIRECTION

YOUR PROTECTION

I LOVE YOU, DADDY

CHAPTER THREE

My Daddy Let Me Know Why I Am Suffering

My daddy let me know why I'm suffering. He said, his children have suffered in the past.

Example One: Sometimes we have suffered in the past because we have said or done something wrong to another person. Our action did not represent the values of my daddy. Then we must experience the same thing later in life.
Sometimes when I say, I am suffering Lord, why is this happening to me. A picture will appear before my eyes. Then I remember the mistake I made. Many times God showed me the wrong I have done. I say, I'm sorry Lord and accept the punishment.

Romans 12:19

Example Number Two: There are times when someone harms you and your plan is to hurt the person too.

One day you plan on hurting the person. God makes you suffer for your wrong.

I understood this one as a kid, so I never use this one. Vengeance is mine saith the Lord.

Example Three: Have you ever had a conversation with someone and God said do not speak and you spoke anyway. After the discussion, you felt frustrated and confused. Because you know what you said is going to hurt you later, you did not listen when God was trying to protect you.

A headache- Frustration is a form of anger.

In such cases my daddy is trying to protect us. But we are failing to obey the Holy Spirit, therefore, we have to suffer. We have brought this suffering on ourselves for not listening to the Holy Spirit. Gn. 3: 10-11

Example: Four: Sometimes it is possible you eat too much pork and your blood pressure is high. You became ill and a family members had to take you to the hospital.

The doctor said you have to stay in hospital for several days until you feel better before you can go home. You are sick and you feel very dizzy. You could have had a stroke or maybe heart attack.

Our body is the temple of God and we have to take care our temples. When we fail to take care of the temple, we suffer. We must live by the word of God.

Example Five: Maybe you are a person who works all the time and who refuses to take the time to rest. You begin to feel like you were under a lot of stress. You made a bad decision, you lack concentration. The decision you made could affect your family or work.

You can not sleep at night and you're not eating the way you should. You're suffering because you're failing to take the time out to get the rest you need. You may experience depression because of your situation, depression lower your spirit. It is anger turned inward.

Moses experience depression. Numbers 11:14

Example Six: If you want, you can buy new clothes all the time, but you can't afford the clothes all the time. You continue to buy clothes on your credit card. Now you can not afford to pay the bills and you never have money. You are depressed all the time.

You are suffering because you are missing one of the fruit of the spirit of self-control with your money.

Galatians 5: 22-23

Seven example: I remember when I was in school and worked at the same time. I did not take the time to read my Bible and pray in the morning. Small things would make me uneasy and frustrated.

If I was driving, and the driver in front of me started to get on my nervous because he did not have his signal light. When I got to work, I had very little patience with my coworkers. I would start to feel stressful.

I am suffering because I stopped eating my spiritual food in the morning. I am weak spiritually.

Example Eight: There may be a time in your life when you know that God calls you to do something and you are refusing to do it. God has been patient and you still refuse to do it. Your life begins to change for the worst.

You are suffering because you refuse to obey God.

Jonah and the Whale
Jonah 1-4

Example Nine: Once I was visiting my friend and it was at night. I got out of my car and I was walking to her apartment building, and the Holy Spirit said, take your credit card, your money, and driver's license out of your bag. When I got to my location, I forgot and thought no more about it.

On the way back to the car, I was walking and there was nobody around me. I never saw anyone behind me or ahead of me. When I got to my car, I did not have my purse. The bag just disappeared.

I knew I had the bag when I left my friend's house. The next day, I did not have any money. I had to renew my driver's license and inform my creditors of my credit cards.

God was trying to protect me, but I was not listening. We must obey the Holy Spirit and we must act when God is speaking to us or we will suffer.

Exdos. 11: 9-11

Example Number Ten:

There are times when we suffer for the glory of God. Maybe you have a loved one who wants to be saved and who is trying to turn his life around. You will stand in the gap until the loved one gives his / her life to Christ.

Mt. 16:21-28

Example Eleven: We suffer when God puts us to the test of faith. We learn patience which is one of the hardest thing to learn.

Galatans. 16: 13

Example Twelve: God allows us to suffer so that we can develop character in us, such as humility, patience and kindness, etc.

Galatans. 5:22-23

First, what happens when you put people, places, and things before God?

These are idolatry in today's time

1. Drugs
2. Alcohol
3. Mind games
4. Money (love of money)
5. Food
6. Sex
7. The relationships

Think back to some hard times in your life, can you remember why you are suffering sometimes in your life?

Answer the following questions

1. Can you remember a time when you were suffering?
    Explain:

2. What lesson did you learn?

3. Why do you belong to God?

    a. Did you forget to remember about how we pay for our bad mistakes?

    b. What did you learn about taking things into your own hands?

4. Did you ever have a conversation and God said do not talk and you did?
    Explain:

5. What did you learn?

6. Have you ever eaten something that was not good for the temple of God?
    Explain:

7. What did you learn about your eating habits?
    Explain

8. Do you do know why you are suffering?

9. Can you remember a time when you made a bad decision?
    Explain

10. What lesson did you learn from your bad decision?

11. Make a list of _____ (idols) you have or you had in you life?

12. What problems happened in your life because ____ (idols)? Explain

13. Do you have a health problem because of _____
    (Idols)? Explan

14. Do you have any close friends that you lost because of your____ (Idols)? Explain

Joural

Start Keeping a journal of your suffering.

Case One: The Problem

What caused the suffering?

What did you learn?

Did you repent?

How do you want to handle this situation? Is it the way of the Lord? He is good.

What is God trying to tell you?

What do you think God wants you to learn?

Case Two: The Problem

What caused the suffering?

Did you repent?

What is God trying to tell you?

What is it that God wants you to learn?

How do you want to handle the situation? Is it the way of the Lord? He is good.

Suffering

Mistakes	1 Samuel. 18:7-1
	Galatians. 6:7-8
The Sin	Gen. 3:14-19
	Lev. 4:1-12
	Jhn. 5:1-14
	Mrk. 7:1-23
	Matt. 8:1-14
	Rom. 3:9-20
The behavior	Gen. 3:1-24
	2 Saumel 11:26-27
	Luke. 12:1-2
	2 Timothy 2:22
The Hidden Sin	Exodus. 2:11-17
	Mattthew 5:27
Punishment	Number 15:30
Temptation	1 Corthians. 10:13
	James. 1:14
	1 Corthians. 10:13
	1 Corthians. 10:13
	James 1:14
Suffering For the Glory of God	Isaish 61:1
	John. 9:2-3
	John 4
Try Our Faith	James 1:2-4
	1 Peter. 4:12-13
Demonstrate Our Relationship	Hebrew. 12:8
	Peter. 3:11-12
For Harvest Producer	Gatians. 5:22-23
	1 Titus 2:12
For Harvest Production	1Corthians 7:1
	Efesians. 1:4
	Hebrews. 12:10
	1Timothy. 3:12

What caused the pain?

What did you learn?

How do you want to handle this? Is it the way of the Lord? He is wonderful.

What do you think God is trying to tell you?

What do you think God wants you learn?

Did you repent?

How do you want to handle the situation? Is it the way of the Lord? He is powerful.

What do you think God is trying to tell you?

What do think God wants you to learn?

Case Three: Problem

What is the reason for your Suffering?

What did you learn?

Did you repent?

Complete the Sentences
1. When I make a mistake I____.
2. I made a mistake and I realized that I ____.
3. Sin is ____.
4. When I sin I ____.
5. 5. My behavior is a sin because____.
6. Anger is __.
7. 7. I like to sin because I ____.
8. 8. There was a time I hid my sin when _____.
9. 9. My behavior is bad when____.
10. 10. I sin when_____.
11. 11. When temptation is present in my life I ____.

January 7, 2014
Saturday 4:20 pm
Thank you Daddy
for
Correcting me
Protecting.

I Love you Daddy.

CHAPTER FOUR

My Self-esteem Comes from My Daddy.

Self-esteem

Is

A

Good Feeling

About What God

Has Done

For You.

February 21, 2014

You Are Looking
at a Nobody
Whom God
Made
Somebody.

Thank You Daddy

Love Your Daughter
Louise

Thank You Daddy,
You
Adopting Me as Your Daughter, I love you.

Thank you Daddy for giving me a since of belongings in this world, you are great.

Daddy you are every special.

Louise

Date: April 7, 1978

NO: 0000001
Certificate of Spiritual Rebirth
A Spiritual Birth
Name: Louise Forshe

Purpose - the old person will die and I will become one new person. 1Corithian 5:17

Romans 8:15 ABBA - Father
I have been adopted by the spirit
this is the Holy Spirit.
I am 34 years old in the Lord.
Location: I am at work.
Comments: Goodbye church member 1959 - March 31, 1978, I am glad about my new birth.

PASSPORT

United States of America

Name Passport: 888000999

Name: Louise Forshe

Spiritual Birth Date

April 1978
State: Illinois U.S.A.
Passport Agency
The Holy Spirit
Given to
Louise Forshe

8 4 2 3 2 7 9 6 0 u s a 7 7 6 5 4 2 1 7 6 2 < < < < < < < < < < < < < < < < < < < < < < < < < < < <
<<_____Signture

Destination: Heaven:

CHAPTER FIVE

DidYou know That My Daddy Told Me That I'm Unique?

The talents and gifts that God has given you is a part of your self-esteem. The talents and gifts you have make you special or unique. The talents people use are like their voice to sing soprano or alto. Examples. Public speaking such as teaching and preaching. Talents are like poetry reading and speed reading.

The Talentes People Use for their Voice are:

The Soprano or the Alto

The Storytelling

Public Speaking

Teaching

Preaching

Using talents of the Hands

The embroidery

Garden work

Cooking

Writing

Painting

Needlepoint

Working With People

Young children

Men or Women

Playing an Instrument

Music

Guitar

Harp   Piano

Flute   Horn

Saxophone

How do I know and can tell, if I have a talent? You may have an interest, or a desire for a gift or talent. It is a gift or talente that need to be developed.

Answers to the following questions:

1. List two of your talents or gifts God gave you that you can use with your hands.
    a.
    b.

2. How do you use these two talents for the glory of God?

3. List two of your talents, God gave you using your voice.
    a.
    b.

4. When was last time you use your voice, which is a talent to glorify God?

5. What musical instrument do you play?

6. How are your musical talents used for the glory of God?

7. How well do you work with the people of the church?

8. List two of your talents or gifts God gave you that you can use with your hands.
    a.
    b.

9. How do you use these two talents to the glory of God?

10. List two of your talents God gave you using your voice?
    a.
    b.

11. When was last time, you use your voice talent to glorify Lord?

12. What is one of your musical instruments that you play?

13. How is your musical talents use for the glory of God?

14. How well do you work with people in the comminity in or outside the church?

15. Which group of people do you work well with?

16. Do you have to develop the talentes God has given you?

17. Do you know you are responsible for developing the talents and gifts God has given you?

The Complete Sentences

1. I'm special ____.
2. He gave me a voice to ____.
3. God allows me to use my hands to____.
4. I work well with people when ____.
5. I serve God with my talents, when ____.
6. I am glad God gave me the gift of_____.

Complete the Sentences

1. I am glad God gave me _____.
2. Because I feel____.
3. When I use this talent, I feel____.
4. I need to develop the gift of _____.

Complete the Sentences

1. I am glad God gave me the talent of____.
2. When I use my talent, it makes me feel__.
3. I like using my talent when__.

One Saturday Morning

January 21 2014

You Made Me Unique.

Thank you daddy, for

a mind to write,

then you also gave me

Teaching Skills,

Counseling skills, and

Speaking skills.

You made me special, when you created me.

God made me special, when he gave me a purpose for

life.

I love you, daddy

Louise

CHAPTER SIX

I Inherited Some of My Daddy's Power

Trust - A strong belief or trust in God.

Gideon - Develop confident in their battle of three hundred soldiers.
Judges 7: 1-25

Paul's confidence grew each time he believed.
1 Corthian 2:15

We must have confidence in God in order to please him.

Brave - The quality of mind or character that makes a person able to face danger.

Examples

John asked for the body of Jesus, so he could give a proper burial. John 10: 38-20: 9

The Mind of determination to follow Christ and do his will.

Samuel, the last judge and most effective prophet. You must have determination to obey God. Israel must get rid of the foreign gods. 1 Samuel 7: 3-17

Faith - The trust that a person has in believing in God. The person will trust God for his needs.

Example

Hannah wanted a child and she had faith. She prayed and prayed until she conceived and gave birth.
1 Samuel 12:21

Flexibility - Easy to change, cooperate, or work with

as Christians. We need to know that our plans will change.

"In his heart a man plans his course, but the Lord determines his step.
Proverbs 16: 9

Hard Working – It is an individual who set a goal and achieve it. He or she can be used by God.

CHAPTER SEVEN

Who Is My Role Model?
My Daddy

The statements are to help you in your spiritual walk with God.

a. God wants to make you his child.
b. Thank God for loving me enough to give me a purpose to help build your kingdom on earth.

   We develop dignity with your assignments.

c. When I am faithful to God, I please God.

Self-love

d. I am made from love and it was the image of God. I am love.
e. I am a gift from the Spirit of God.

Self-esteem

f. When I know, I'm standing in the power of God. I am capable of the work he has assigned me.

Self-assured

g. The God I trust, it makes my faith increase.

Bravery

h. The Lord always guide me, when I ask him to show me the way.

Self-esteem

i. God loves me, therefore it allows me to do the work of my Father.

Determining

j. Lord, when I grow in my spiritual walk with you, it makes me happy.

Self-esteem

k. I'm a nice person because I have a part of the glory of God in me.

Self-esteem

l. God, when I talk to you and the more I listen to you the more joy I feel in my soul.

Self-esteem

m. The more I live by God's values the closer I feel to you.
n. When the spirit of God touches my body, I know I am loved.

Self-esteem

o. I will find true happiness.

Determination

p. Take an affirmation and repeat it for thirty days. Then if you feel you have developed or increase in that area, take another statement and repeat the same statement for another thirty days.

A special prayer
For
Spiritual Growth

a. Lord, please heal my insecurities, so I can be used by you.
b. God I am vulnerable in some areas of my life.

Please heal me in those areas and make me strong.

Things to Remember

c. When your spirit is broken, and you have a lack of confidence. You feel weak in your prayer life. Ask God for strenght.
d. When you want to rebuild your self- confidence, you can ask God to rebuild your confidence. Tell God you want to please him and give him your best. You need self-confidence that comes from His Spirit.

A Prayer for Your Mentor

e. God always let me see the God in this person.

CHAPTER EIGHT

Did You Know That My Daddy Said Affirmations Are Spiritual Food For the Soul?

My daddy is a spirit that formed himself into a man to come to earth. God called himself Jesus when he walked the earth. God loves me very much. He died for our sins. Because of my daddy flesh, I learned to think, act, and have control of myself.

My daddy wants us to teach and share with others as Jesus did.

1. Repentance, ask God to forgive you for your wrong.

We repent when we have done wrong, and share with others how important it is to ask God to forgive us. Matthew 4:17

When a person repents he should talk to the Lord.

I'm sorry, please forgive me. King David repented every time he did wrong. II Samuel

What does repentance do to my spirit?

A. The individual gives up the sin.
B. The person is becoming more like God.
C. It gives you an opportunity to have a closer walk with God.
D. The individual behavior will start to change.

Repenting of your sin, you have peace and your spirit is free. You can experience self-esteem, and increase your self- esteem. You will feel closer to Him as you read or reread the stories about him. It will help you want to please him in your walk with him. The stories will help you want to repent when you need to. It will help you know that God is a forgiving God. Lastly, it will help you want to be closer to him after you repent.

1. Jesus is theMessiah.
    a. Messiah means anointed by God. Matt. 12:28
    b. The power and wisdom of God. 1 Cor. 1: 23-24
    c. He is The Suffering Servant. Isaiah 53:12
    d. You will learn to believe the messages and the miracles of my daddy.

Jesus healed a crippled man who could not walk.

The man was crippled for many years. He put him in the Pool of Bethesda. John. 5:1-18

Jesus uses teachers. The teachers want you to learn, so you can understand. Jesus is concerned about the people.

Jesus was a preacher. He was concerned about people being committed to the father. He wants us to be faithful as well.

Jesus healing the sick, he was concern about the total body. He healed people physically, mentally and spiritually.

When you think about how Jesus was concerned about people, it gives him honor. Honor develops dignity in people always. Their concern should show love for people. He teaches us how to respect him and his father. So we can learn to respect each other and ourselves.

Complete the Sentences

1. When I heard the name Jesus_____.
2. Jesus made a blind man see and I _____.
3. Jesus walked on water and I _____.

When I think about how I care for my Jesus ___.

1. The heart of Jesus is
   a. He healed a man with leprosy. Matthew 8: 1-4
   b. Jesus calms the wind. Matthew 8: 23-27
   c. Jesus healed a man named. Legion.
   d. Legions are demons or evil spirits.
   e. Jesus walking on water. Matthew 14: 33-36
   f. Jesus makes the blind man see. John 9: 35-41
   g. Jesus love the little children. Matthew 19:14
   h. Jesus raised Lazarus from the dead. John 11:38-44

When you read these stories it gives you hope. We learn to believe and trust God for ourself. These stories can relieve depression and your spirit is free of negative emotions. Just because you have hope and your spirit is up, remember hope develops trust in God. If you trust God you will feel close to God. Your self-esteem will increased.

Fill in the Blank

My daddy walks this earth _____ thousand years.

He was in Bethlehem when he ____ ____. He is _____.

I want you to believe in my daddy.

He was called_____.

The Messiah is_____.

My father was his mother's _____ child.

Jesus had_____ brothers and their names were_____.

Mt. 13:55

He love the little _____. He will be with _____ in good or _____ times.

To be like my daddy, you _____. We must _____ our neighbor.

CHAPTER NINE

Did You Read Some of My Daddy's Life Lessons from the Biblical Time that My Daddy Left Behind?

There are many great stories of the Bible that helps you with life lessons today. We can avoid consequences in your life.

Abraham and Sarah - The first stepfamily Gn. 16
It was the consequences of bad decisions Gn. 21: 8-21

Daniel - The Prayer Warrior Daniel. 6:10 - 23

King David – When he had sinned he repented.

2 Samuel 12

Esther - When her life was in danger, she prayed first.

Esther 4

Isaac and Rebekah - Favoritism Genesis. 25:28

Jeremiah – His difficult task. 19

Jesus -Resolve problems and demonstrate people skills.
Luke. 6: 43-45

John the Baptist - His testimony to prove he was the forerunner for Christ. Matthew 3

Jonah - The consequences for disobeying God
Jonah. 1-4

Noah - Determine to finish the work at all costs for God.
Genesis 6

Apostle Paul - Saul preached about Christ. He escaped death.
We have a Purpose in Life.

Adam - The First Zoologist

Named all the animals Genesis. 2:19

Animals also have a spiritual meaning.

Lion - real power and strength
Proverbs 30:30

Bear - Great Courage 1 Samuel 17: 3-4

Sparrow - Free from anxiety
Matthew 10: 29-30

Owl – Loneliness Psalm 102: 6-7

Wolf - Order and Unity
Genesis 49:27

War Horse - Force to mock fear
Job 39: 19-25

CHAPTER TEN

My Dad Wants You to Enjoy the Fruits of the Spirit

LOVE JOY

PEACE

LONG SUFFERING

MEEKNESS

GOODNESS

FAITH KINDNESS

PATIENCE

FRUIT OF THE SPIRIT

Love - Affection, Commitment, Compassion

The affection – It's like a warm, loving feeling to follow up of an action.

Proverbs 4:23

Example: God blessed me today because he sent someone to give me a hug. God knew I needed a hug. He told the person to tell me that God loves me. He really loves you.

Commitment - A pledge or promise, faithfulness

Psalm 37:5

Example: Every Christian needs to make a promise to God to live by his principles and values through the word of God.

Compassion - The feeling of having understanding for others, the desire to help and show kindness.

Job 6:14

Compassion is the understanding of personal needs and help a person in need.

Example: A new member of my church, needs some clothes to wear to church. I'll share some of my clothes with her.

Love comes from God.

God is love. 1 John. 4:16

Love is a blessing to others. 1Cor. 13: 4-7

Love is a gift from God.

When we love, we have the following attributes that come from God.

Love for others

Example: A friend was homeless and a member of a church took her in.

Love comes from God.

God is love. 1 John. 4:16

Love is a blessing to others. 1Cor. 13: 4-7

Love is a gift from God and it comes from his image.

When we love we have the following attributes that come from God.

- Forgiveness of oneself, knowing that God is a forgiving God.
- It is the understanding and patience with others and self.
- You have decided to do the will of God.

Joy - Blessing and joy

Contentment - happy and satisfied

Joy comes from God when we trust him.

Philippians 4:12

Content is being happy with what you have.

Example: You have family problems, but you are satisfied or have peace. It is because you believe that God will work the problems out.

Delight —It is great pleasure and rejoicing when the individual is happy, or satisfied.

Happy is to find a deeper way of hope and joy.
Matthew 5: 11-12

Joy in the Lord, - He shall give you the desires of your heart.
Psalm 37:4

Have a deep hope and joy for God.

Example: The love of God gives a new Christian great joy.

Laughter - the sound of joy.

What is the sound of joy, peace, happiness?

Peace is being calm.

Peace is calm and rest and being satisfied.

Joy – gladness and delight

When we have joy, it is because it comes from God. We have a special attribute.

The Holy Spirit is the Presence of God.

We can experience the presence of God in worship.

We can experience true worship.

Patience grows as we help others.

Calm – I want you to think of the sea on a warm summer day.

You'll find peace.

We must never take advantage of the patience of God.

Joshua 23:16

Example: Christian shows us that we can trust God. It is when we can not see the way through the situation. We can be calm because we still have joy.

Silence – quiet and no movement

Affection – It's like a warm feel. You will feel loved followed by action. Prov. 4:23

Example: God blessed me today because God gave me a hug.

God loves everyone.

Commitment - A pledge or promise

Psalm 37: 5.

EXAMPLE: Every Christian needs to make a promise to God to live by HIS principles and valúes through the word of God.

Commitment – Care, Support, and Kindness, a pledge to do something or give a promise to be faithful to someone or something.

CHAPTER ELEVEN

I have Some of My Daddy's Glory

Wednesday 2:00 pm April 8, 2014

Daddy, I feel so special

to have something of your glory.

Your Glory

Your Honor   Your Beauty

Your Power

Jesus Is My Glory.

Thank You!

He is Special:

Example: God blessed me today because he knew I needed a hug. He hug me with his spirit.

When we love, we have the following attributes that comes from God.

Self-love   Love for others

Understanding of myself

Understanding of Other   Patience for myself and others

I am determine to do the will of God.

When Christians cannot be themselves, problems will come. We are going to experience stress.

It indicates that we are not trusting God with all your heart. Exodus 16: 2

Remember when we experience stress in our lives. We should pray all the time. Read Psalm 62: 1-2.

When we have peace, we have inherited many of the attributes of God.

Trust in God

I am happy because God lives in me.

I have joy.

Joy-happiness, goodness, and blessing

Contentment - peace and happiness

Contentment comes from God when we trust in Him.

Phil. 4:12

Content is enjoying something in your life.

Example: You have a problem with the family, but you're happy or you have peace, because you believe that God will work the problems out.

Delight – It is being happy or satisfied.

Happy is to find hope and joy.

The joy of the Lord. He will give you the desires of your heart. We have hope and joy in the Lord.

Example: A new Christian, the love of God gives a new Christian blessings right away. God want them to believe and trust Him.

Laughter - The sound of laughing is the sound of joy, peace, happiness. The peace is a sign of joy Lev. 23: 1-2

Peace is calm, rest and silence

Example: Peace will come when we obey God.

When we have the joy that comes from God, we have a special attribute. The Holy Spirit is our guide.

We are happy no matter what comes our way. We must understand and experience true worship. True worship is when your mind is on Jesus and you are renewing the truth about our heavenly Father.

Patience- to grow and let others grow.

Peace- calm, silence, and rest

Calm is think of the sea and a quiet summer day.

Calm is a way of patience. We must never take

advantage of the patience of God.

Joshua 23:16

Example: It shows Christians that they can trust in God no matter how painful the situation maybe. We have joy because God is our hope. Silence – quiet and no movement. Hebrews 4: 9-11

Christians can not hear from God many times until they are silent. When Christians are in a battle, we must know that God is present.

Example: When Christians are silent they receive the wisdom of God. They also receive God's interaction and messages to the problem in their life.

We need to relax our physical bodies, so that we can be at peace while our emotions are calm. It will help us be consistent with our worship.

We must rest so we can have the power in our spirit to worship God. Rest is sleep and relaxation. God allows us to rest.

Example: Sometimes when christians rest, they are preparing for battle. It's one of the things Christians need to learn how to do. We must know how to fight in battle. Hebrew. 4: 1-13

The Relaxation - to do or become less firm. When Christians stop being themselves daily, problem comes, they experience stress.

Tension - indicate we are not trusting God with all our heart. Exodus 16: 2.

Remember when we experience stress in our lives we must pray, read the Bible, and believe. Psalm 62: 1-2. When we have peace, we have inherited many of the attributes of God. Trust God and be happy because God lives in us.

Joy is being happy in our mind, heart, and soul.

What is the cause our joy and happiness?

We know that Jesus is the cause of our joy and happiness.

When we have joy, we can show mercy to other.

When we have joy we have patience and we can be a good listener.

Long suffering - Patience

We can take our time, we must grow in God.

We need to grow in God. We can let others

grow in God, if we are patience. God is patience

with us that is one way he shows his love.

Meekness develops the attributes of God as:

    a. Developing discipline and a balance in the mind.
    b. Change our hearts to love when necessary.
    c. Be kind to others.
    d. Help develop good listening skills.
    e. Goodness - best, positive, right

The best - desirable, excellency, the best that we can be.

God wants our best in serving Him.

When we serve others and give others our best, it is the best way to become like Christ. Rm. 7: 6

Positive - It is important to have a positive attitude when we are serving God.

Attitude - thinking, acting and feeling.

A positive attitude can mean allowing God to prepare you for a great assignment for him.

Genesis. 39:21

You will be a great example for others who serve God.

Right - You live by God values. As a servant, you live by representing the values of God.

Example: An individual who stands to represent Christ, no matter if everyone is against you. You need to stand for what is right.

kindness is the product of God's attributes.

Apostle Paul said, God is first and always.

a. The positive attitude
b. Defend what is right.
c. Develop dignity by doing a good work for God.
d. Develop self-esteem because God made you from his spirit.
e. You feel good about your self-worth, which is based on God's love that he has for you.

Faith - belief and trust

When you believe, it must come from the heart. It must be accepted by God. Roman 10: 9

Believing is an action. Genesis. 15: 6

Example: Christians must believe the word of God that he is God.

God will allow our faith to grow in the situation

Of the problem. (How will we grow?)

a. Trust - assurance and boldness
b. Warranty - Security
c. Security is based on the word of God.

When we are guarantee, it is the way of our heavenly father. God takes care of his children.

Security - Christians feel comfort in Christ.

Christians know that there is safety in Christ.

We know that God will protect us every day.

The Apostle Paul boldly witness to others to win souls for Christ. Example, Christians must learn how to stand up and spread the word of God boldly to the unbeliever.

Trust is believing in God. When we develop trust, it will represent one of the attributes of God.

1. Trust is based on courage.
2. Build faith
3. Learn to believe in God.
4. It makes you stand on the Word of God.
5. It removes the fear.
6. It develops security in God.
7. It will help develop or increase life expectancy.

Meekness is patience and it is slow to get angry. The individual will be learning how to be very humble.

Humble- It is when we are free from pride and arrogance. You also know who you are in Christ.

Christians who are humble learn to pray for what they really want. They are very consistent in prayer.

God's people need to learn how to be humble in order to be a good servant.

Example: Sometimes Christians do things for Christ but do not have the humility.

God uses situations to develop humility in his children.

CHAPTER TWELVE

Leadership

The President of the United States, the House of Representatives, Senators and public leaders we need to pray for them.

Your great love you have in mind, and always walk in your truth.

Psalms 26: 3

Whatever you do, work heartily as working for the Lord, and not for anyone in this world.

Colossians 3:23

The President of the United States, the House of Representatives, and senators need prayer and the Word of God. Here are some Scriptures that will make you think and pray for our government leaders.

Your great love You have in mind, and always walk in your truth. Psalms 26: 3

The Lord God is my strength: He makes my feet like the feet of a gazelle and my feet like a deer.

Habakkuk 3:19

GOD CALLS THE COMMON PEOPLE

God uses ordinary people. God uses all kinds of people to do a job.

Jacob - A liar	Genesis 27
Jospeh - A slave	Genesis 39-47
Moses - A shepherd in exile	Exdus 4:19
Gideon - A farmer	Judges. 6:11
Jephthah - The child of a prostitute	Judges. 11: 1
Hannah - a housewife	1 Samuel 1
Esther - an orphan	Esther 2:7
Mary - a peasant girl	Luke 1: 28-38
Mother of Christ	Luke 1: 27-38
Matthew - A tax collector	Matthew 9: 9
Luke - a Greek physician	Colossians 4:14

Peter - A fisherman   Matthew 4: 18-20

No one is perfect and we will never be perfect. It is important that we grow and mature in Jesus Christ.

What do you contribute as a leader?

__ Understanding Psalm 119: 34   __ Listening skills Dt 5: 1.
__ Honesty Isa. 33: 14-16   __Courage 2 Cor. 5:10
__ Discipline. Gal. 5: 16-26   __ Responsibility Proverbs 24: 11-12.
__ Tolerance Rom. 14: 1-10   __ Vision Mt 19: 16-30
__ Integrity Pr 28: 6.   __ Respect Pr 9:10.
__ Resistance Jr. 29: 1-14   __ Compassion Mt. 14:14
__ Commitment Mt. 13: 18-23   __ Enthusiasm Eph. 6:5
__ Humility Mrk. 9: 33-35   __ Patience Zep. 1:19
__ Faithful Mt. 26: 3   __Forgiveness Mt. 18: 21-22
__ Passion 1 Sam.l 17: 39-52   __ Refuge Pr. 22: 3
__ Integrity Ps. 78:72   __ Meekness Ps. 62: 5
__ Justice Mt. 7: 2   __ Gratitude 1 Cor 4: 7
__ Truth Jn. 14: 1   __ Wisdom 1 PR. 3: 9
__ Self-sacrifice Mk. 10: 42-45   __ Creative 1 Timothy. 4:14
__ Efficient 1 Pet. 4:10   __ Availability Mk. 1: 17-18

What do you need to work on as a leader? Put a check mark by each one.

What are your transfer skills that will help you as a leader?

Examples: Working with women

Working with children

1.

2.

3.

4.

What are you skills from being a VIP that you can still use for this job?

1.
2.
3.
4.
5.

What are your spiritual gifts that you can use as a leader?

Romans 12 1 Corinthians 12

Exhortation

Administration

Giving 1 Corinthians 12: 1-11

Leadership

Discernment _

Mercy -

Help _

Healing Services _

Teaching Knowledge of Miracles _ Ephesians 4:11

Prophecy _

Apostle _

Education _

Evangelization _

Dr. Arie Louise Forshe, Ph.D., MSW

Pastor_

Wisdom _

Speaking in Tongues _

Interpretation _

Esther Was an Ordinary Person

Esther Strengths and Talents in Time of Trouble

The Book of Esther

She lives by example: 4:16

Together they Fasted faithfully 4: 12-14

An open mind 4:15

(She heard Mordecai)

Acceptance of the event 4: 15-16

Intercessor 4:16

Courage to go to the king 5:10

Faith in God 4: 16b

Organization 5: 3-5

Creativity - banquet 5: 4

Patience - second banquet 5: 8

Honesty 7: 3-4

Assertive 7: 5-6

Faithful (her people) 4:16

What are some of your strengths and skills? Here are some possibilities.

1. Ability to listen   Deuteronomy 5:1
2. Availability   Mark. 1: 17-18
3. Commitment   Matthew 13: 18-23
4. Believe and trust God   Colossians 1: 10

5. Justice   Matthew 7: 2
6. Forgiving   Matthew 18: 21-22
7. Gratitude   1 Corinthians 47
8. Humility   Mark 9: 33-35

Today, I have a problem.

What strengths or skills will you use to solve this problem?

An Open Mind

Honesty   Organization

Creativity

The self-control

Advocate

Faith in God

1.
2.
3.
4.

CHAPTER THIRTEEN

What happened?

Life is filled with individual lessons. If you do not learn the lessons the first time, the lessons are repeated.

Exodus 5:1-2

God promised the people they would be released.

1. "Then Moses and Aaron went to Pharaoh and said, Lord God of Israel, says: Let my people go to celebrate a feast in the desert. 2. And Pharaoh said, who is your Lord that I should obey his voice to let the Israelites go? I know not the Lord, nor let the Israelites go.

Conquences Begin

Ex. 7: 4-22 - The Plague of Blood

Ex. 8: 1-15 - The Plague of Frogs

Ex. 8: 20-32 - The Plague of Flies

Ex. 9: 1-7 – The Plaage Cattle

Ex. 9: 8-12 - The Plague Boils

Ex. 9: 13-35 - The Plague Hail

Ex. 10: 1-20 - The Plague Locusts

Ex. 10: 20-29 - The Plague Darkness

Ex. 11: 1-10 - The Plague Firstborn

What do you thing God wanted the Pharaoh to learn?

What are the lessons God wants you to learn?

How many times do you have to repeat the lesson before you understand what God want you to learn?

THE MIND GAMES PEOPLE PLAY

The mind games that people play at work and even in our churches.

Genesis. 27:27

Jacob deceived Esau of his birthright and blessings. Laban, Jacob's uncle told him if he works for seven years, he could marry his youngest daughter Rachel. Jacob worked seven years and his uncle told him he could not have Rachel. But instead, he tricked him and gave him Leah his oldest daughter. Jacob never learned to truely love her. Laban was not a man of his word. He told him, you would have to work another seven years for Rachel. Jacob worked another seven years, so he could marry Rachel.

Jacob, and his uncle Laban had a problem.

Principle number one: You treat people the way you want to be treated. It is the second greatest commanmant.

Rape

Tamar was the daughter of King David. She had a brother and her brother name was Absalom and a half brother name Ammon. Amnon fail in love with his half sister Tamar. He wanted to take her to bed. His friend told him to pretend that he was sick. When your father King David comes to visit you, ask your father to let Tamar come and cook for you. Ammon took his friend's advice. His friend was his cousin. He was King David's nephew. His name was Jonadab.

King David spoke with his daughter Tamar about visiting her brother because he was sick. She went and cooked for him. Ammon sent all his servants away. When she brought the food, Ammon forced his sister on the bed and raped her.

After he raped her, he hated her more than he loved her. She was put out of his home. Absalom learned what Ammon had done to his sister. He tells her to keep quiet. King David learned what his oldest son has done. He was very angry.

Two years later Absalom had a sheep shearing. Absalom asked his father if his brothers could come. Absalom made a plan. He had his half brother Ammon killed for raping his sister.

King David learned that Ammon was dead. King David was upset for a long time. Absalom fled to Geshur.

2 Samuel 13

What are some of the things Tamar may have experienced as a rape victim? Example: a. Sadness b. isolation c. a loss of interest in things that were meaning to her.

1.

2.

3.

4.

5.

6.

7.

Scriptures of Comfort

Physical Abuse

Col. 3:19
Eph. 5:21
Jn. 10:10
Phil. 2: 4

Eat Excessively

Lk. 7:34
Lk. 21:34

Verbal Abuse

Ps. 57: 4.

Manipulation

MT4: 57
Lk. 14:11
Ex. 16: 14-16

Widow

Adapt to a New Lifestyle

Tamar Gn. 37-38
Naomi Ruth 1: 3-5.
Zeruah 1kgs. 11: 26-31
Anna Lk. 2: 36-38

Ruth RT 2: 2.
Orpah. Rt 1: 4.

People in the Bible Who Experience Depression

Moses Numbers. 11:15
Jonah - Jonah. 4: 3
Elijah - 1kings. 19: 4
Isaiah - 6: 5.
Saul - 1Samuel 28:13
Mordecai - Esther 4: 1-7.
Mary Magdalene- John. 20:13

Incest

Genesis 19: 30-38
1 Chronicles. 5: 1

Rape

Genesis 19:18
Genesis. 34: 27-29

Sex

Deuteronoy 23:17-18
PR. 5: 18-20
1Cor. 7:35
1Cor. 7: 9
1 Tim. 4: 8

Money Addict

2kgs. 5: 20-27
2Chr. 25: 9-10
Pr. 18:11
Ec. 10:19
Mt 18: 30
Mk. 11: 15-17
MT. 23: 13-14
Mk. 10:26
Lk 6:35
Lk. 18: 24-27

Alcoholishm

Gn.9: 20-27
Est. 1: 10-10
Pr. 23: 29-30
Pr.3: 4-7

Prejudice

Gn.5:35 Jos 4:4

CHAPTER FOURTEEN

A Life Without the Balance

Remember

There is a balance in everything.

Exercise - Are you trying to make your problems?

There is a balance in everything. Exercise - Are you trying to make your problems disappear?

"For bodily exercise it is profitable too little."

1 Timothy 4: 8

Glutton - Are you eating foods to removes your pain?

The son of man comes eating and drinking, and you say a friend to a tax collector or a sinner. Luke 7:34

"Let your hearts weighed down with dissipation and drunkenness, and cares of this world.

Luke 21:34

Do want sex every day? Do you need sex daily?

"You have heard that it was said, Thou shalt not commit adultery." But I tell you that anyone who looks at a woman lustfully has already committed adultery with her in his heart.

Matthew 5: 27-28

Your Voice - Use you authority

My soul is among lions: I lie among them that are set on fire, whose teeth are spears and arrows, and their tongue a sharp sword

Psalm 57: 4

Money - Does money control your decisions?
(Main Source)

"For the love of money is a root of all kinds of evil. Some people, eager for money, have wandered from the faith and pierced themselves with many griefs.

1 Timothy 6:10

Do you have a problem with sex?

Gn. 34: 27-29 Genesis. 39: 9
Deut. 23: 17-18 Pr 5: 3. Prov. 6: 25-35
1 Ts 4:18 Pr. 7:25-28
Rom. 1:26-27 1 Co. 6:13
Pr. 2:20 1 c. 6:19-20
Lv. 20:10-21
Pr.. 2:16
Rom. 1:26-27
Pr. 2:20
1Cor. 7:35

Do you have a problem with money?

2 Kgs. 5:20-27 Mk. 10:17-23
2 Cor.25:9-10 Mk. 10:26
Psa.. 37:27 Lk. 6:35
Pr. 18:1 Lk. 18:24-27
Ecc. 10:19
Mt. 18:30
MK. 11:15-17
Mt. 23:13-14

The comfort of the body

Col. 3:19
Ef. 5:21
Jn. 10:10
Fil. 2:4

Glutton

Lk. 7:34
Lk. 21:34

A problem with the voice

Psalm 57: 4.
Proverbs 23: 29-30.
PR.4 7

Do you have a problem with drinking alcohol?

Gn. 9: 20-27
Est. 1: 10-10
Proverbs 23: 29-30.
PR.4 7

The violation of another person's body
(Sex)

Gn. 19:18
Gn. 34:27

Sex Issues

Gn. 34:27-28 Gn. 39:9 Lv. 20:10-21
Dt. 23:17-18 Jue 16:15 Pr. 21:16
Pr. 5:3 Pr. 6:25-35 Ro. 1:26-27
1 Ts. 4:18 Pr. 7:25-28 Mt. 57-28
1 Co. 6:13 Pr. 2:20 1 Co. 6:19-20
1 Co. 7:35

CHAPTER FIFTEEN

Letters

Date: February 27, 2015

Thanks Daddy for making me a substance abuse counselor volunteer in November 1984. In 1985, I became a counselor to work with women after that, I started counseling in other areas in the field. I had my own private practice for ten years. I did well until there was a famine in the U.S.

Daddy the house I lived in for twenty six years and one month, it was from October of 1987, to November 2013. I believe it will be a counseling center. The address of my house is 658 Keep Ave. Elgin, IL 60120 on the eastside of town. I believe in my heart, it will help many people.

Love Louise

Date February 27, 2015

Dear Daddy,

In August 1998, I attended a women's conference the next month I was supposed to begin teaching in a Bible school. I was just a counselor and the other teachers were pastors, ministers, and one has a doctor of theology.

I was afraid, I prayed to my Daddy. I said everyone in the room was told to pray. The prophecy went force, and a lady told me I have spent lots of time with you. I have prepared you. I have ordained you to teach the word of God, thus said the Lord, now go teach.

Thank you daddy!
Love Louise

Date: February 2015

Thanks Daddy for
Louise Ministry Forshe
LOUISE FORSHE MINISTRIES 2000- 2013

The foundation of these ministries is based on 1 Corinthians 12: 27-28

27 Now you are the body of Christ and individually members of it. 28 And in the church God has appointed first apostles; secondly, prophets; thirdly, teachers; then, Miracles; then gifts of healing, **helps**, administrations, various kinds of tongues.

The Women Ministry - We gave food and infant clothing. We gave clothes, diapers, food, milk, and shampoo for babies to young mothers.

Men Minstry - Men's Cologne and seminars and conferences

The Elderly Ministry -, chocolate candy, cookies, depends and conducted church sevices, and preached the Word of God.

Children Ministry – School supplies, outing with games and they had fun as they learned about God.

Spanish-English Bibles were pasted out.

Scholarship Mininstry

One time we were able to give a grant - $500.00 to enter a local Junior college 2010

Mother's Day Seminars – we gave each individual mother a gift for Mother's Day and had a Mother's Day conference each year. 2001-2006

2000-2013 - Prison Ministry - Letters were mailed to the jails and prisons in the fifty states of the U.S.

Women seminars and conferences in the community. We gave a Family's Day conference once.

In 2001, the ministry became English and Spanish.

God has this ministries on hold for now.
www.pastordrlouiseforshe.org

Thank You Daddy
Love Your Daughter Louise

Date: February 28, 2015

Thanks Daddy for June 2004, I became a pastor of a church. You are wonderful. I learned that it was hardly any African American female pastors of a church in the area at that time.

Daddy you told me to learn Spanish, Polish, French, and Swahili. You wanted me to learn to preach, pray, and praise you in these languages. There were no other churches in the area or surrounding area that held there services in these five languages. This is an unique kind of church. I feel, so blessed you picked me to be the pastor of this church.

Thank You Daddy!

Love Your Daughter
Louise

Date: March 3, 2015

Dear Daddy,

I'm glad you put me on the radio.
It is my small radio station 5/2012. www.spreaker.com
I preached in English and Spanish at the same time. 1/2007
English and Swahili 12/2007
English and Polish 2008, and praise you in
English and French 2010. You taught me how to
do both at the same time. It is a special way of
preaching. I was the first one in my area and
surrounding to preach this way. I can preach a twenty minitues
message using all five lanugages in that one message.

Thank you Daddy

The dates have been changed in the following letters below.

January 6, 2014

Dear Daddy,

I love you, I can talk to you any time I feel I want to or I need to. I never have to wait until you get home. I always know how to reach you.

Daddy I need a car. Daddy, thanks for the things you gave me this week.

Love
Louise

Thanks Daddy you're great because of your courage. You gave me courage.

In September of 2010, during the time I was unemployed because I had worked in private practice for ten years and I did well. But after that time I did not make enough money to make end meet due to economy. I wanted to continue to learn Spanish, but I did not have enough money to take a Spanish Class.

One day when I came to the local library, I saw a group of Latinos students in one of the conference room. I learned that it was a English Class. I went into the classroom and looked at the teacher and the class, then I said, I want to learn Spanish. The teacher looked at the class and then she looked at me. She said this is a English Class. I said, I want to learn Spanish. The teacher repeated herself and I repeated myself. Then she said have a seat. Today the class is bilingual.

Thanks Daddy, for loving me and giving me so many of your attributes. Thanks for showing me love, compassion, and grace this week. Daddy thank you for showing me how to raise my spirit with the fruit of the spirit. Thank you God for doing things for me.

Love
Louise

January 12, 2014

Dear Daddy,

I remembered back in January when I asked for dates that would help me coordinate a seminar for the year. I wanted these dates so we would be able to meet.

I Needed the people in the community to attend the seminar. I am asking for October 9, of this year. Daddy, let me remind you that I was born on this day. I wanted to spend this weekend watching you bless others.

When I say bless, I mean, change people lifestyles. I feel you should be blessed on my birthday because you let me live another year. Daddy, I want to be a blessing for you this weekend as well.

Love Louise

February 20, 2014

Dear Daddy,

You know I was in the church today and I felt, I needed an answer about my situation. I went to the bathroom and I began to pray. My Daddy knows I wanted to give my best and do my best. Before I finished praying, God had changed my situation. Then there was an altar call but God had answered my prayer.

I went to the altar and began to talk to my daddy. I heard him say I have answer your prayer. I said, thank you Lord. After I dried the tears from my eyes. I had to say thank you Daddy.

Love
Louise

Febrary 26, 2014

Dear Daddy,

Thanks for waking me up early in the morning 2:00 a.m. in the midnight hour. Thank you also for speaking in my mind during the day.

Daddy you think enough of me to use me to write this book. Daddy you are awesome because you used my skills to allow me to learn. You spoke on my level of education. You talk on the level of your children.

Daddy, I know you could have given this assignment to another person, but you gave it to me, I love you daddy. This assignment makes me feel so special. Thanks daddy, for this assignment. You gave me the dignity, values and increase my confidence to write this book.

Love
Your daughter
Louise

October 9, 2014

Dear Daddy,

Thank you for allowing me to live another year. Today is my birthday as you already know. Daddy I want to be a blessing to you on my birthday. At the 7:00 pm night service, there will be a seminar for families. God bless the families here in the seminar. Let your light shine through me when I speak and pray tonight.

I will give you the honor, praise and glory. Then on Sunday at 9:00 am, I will speak blessings into the families homes. Daddy please touch young people and the elderly in the world. Give them a desire to want to know who you are. On Monday, I'm going to take a tour to one of the local nursing homes.

I love you
Your Daughter Louise

October 11, 2014

Dear Daddy,

Daddy is there something else I can do for you this week. I love you Daddy, you're so good to me. You make me feel so special by the way you care for me.

Daddy, I want to always be faithful to you. Daddy, I want to show you that I have a deep love for you, too. I really hope that I am acceptable in your eyes. I like calling you daddy.

Love
Your daughter

Louise

DADDY, I LOVE YOU
PLEASE HELP ME
KEEP MY EYES AND MIND
FOCUS ON YOU. I WANT TO BE THE
APPLE YOUR EYES.

THANKS DADDY FOR THIS ASSIGNMENT

Now Daddy if you are finished using me, prepare me for the next assignment. Daddy give me what I need, so I'll be ready for next time. Daddy, you are my first love.

I have tried to be obedient to you and live by your word. I hope I'm pleasing to you. Please tell me if I'm not pleasing to you. I do not want my work in vain. Daddy, I want to hear you say one day well done.

Printed in the United States
By Bookmasters